DESIGN CHALLENGE:

Pyramids Plus!

BY SHARYN SQUIER CRAIG

CHITRA PUBLICATIONS
Your Best Value in Quilting

Chitra Publications
2 Public Avenue
Montrose, Pennsylvania 18801

Second Printing: 1997

Library of Congress Cataloging-in-Publication Data

Craig, Sharyn Squier, 1947-
    Design challenge : pyramids plus! / by Sharyn Squier Craig.
        p.   cm.
    ISBN 1-885588-16-X
    1. Patchwork--Patterns.   2. Strip quilting.   3. Machine quilting.
4. Patchwork quilts.   I. Title.
TT835. C726 1997
746.46'041--dc21   97-17382
                                                                    CIP

Editors: Nancy Roberts and Joyce Libal
Design and Illustrations: Susan Barefoot
Cover Photography: Guy Cali Associates, Inc., Clarks Summit, PA
Inside Photography: Ken Jacques Photography, San Diego, CA,
Van Zandbergen Photography, Brackney, PA and Craige's Photography, Montrose, PA

The quilt rack on the front cover was graciously supplied by:
Jasmine Heirlooms, 500 Fairview Drive, Greenville, SC 29609
Phone: (864) 292-0735 or (800) 736-7326

The headboard on the front cover was graciously supplied by:
Lee's Furniture, 26 Church Street, Montrose, PA 18801
Phone: (717) 278-3711

Quilts on the back cover were made by Karen Stanton and
Yong Hui Torske (Center) and Ruth Gordy (bottom).

Our Mission Statement:
We publish quality quilting magazines and books that recognize, promote and inspire self-expression. We are dedicated to serving our customers with respect, kindness and efficiency.

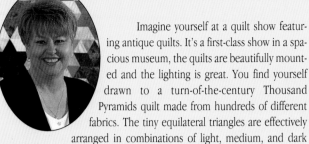

Imagine yourself at a quilt show featuring antique quilts. It's a first-class show in a spacious museum, the quilts are beautifully mounted and the lighting is great. You find yourself drawn to a turn-of-the-century Thousand Pyramids quilt made from hundreds of different fabrics. The tiny equilateral triangles are effectively arranged in combinations of light, medium, and dark values so that your eye constantly refocuses on dozens of different overlapping pyramids. You find yourself gazing at big ones and little ones, mesmerized by the small jewel-like shapes exploding on the surface.

If you're like me, you find yourself wondering "How did the quiltmaker do that?" as you stand before this magnificent quilt. How did our grandmothers figure out how to cut and piece those triangles to create such wonderful pyramid designs? They didn't have fancy quilt shows, shops that hold classes or hundreds of books full of glorious pictures to inspire them. They didn't own yards-upon-yards of fabric to work with. I'll probably never know how they came up with their designs or how they devised cutting and piecing strategies. But I do know this aspect of making a quilt has always intrigued me.

"How can I most efficiently cut and piece this quilt?" is the question that has sparked many of my Design Challenges. The Thousand Pyramids is no exception. When a student casually asked if I knew any strip methods for making a Thousand Pyramids quilt, I had to answer, "No." At the time, I wasn't interested in the pattern. You see, I am not drawn to patterns in which there is only one way to arrange the design units. I prefer those with more design potential—which I didn't think was possible with the triangles used in the Thousand Pyramids.

Her innocent question prompted me to look for an easy sewing system to make units for this pattern. Developing the system allowed me to make my version of a Thousand Pyramids quilt. While I worked, I thought about other designs that could be created with the units. Besides, the cutting and sewing system was too much fun to be used for just one quilt! You can probably guess what happened next. The Pyramids Plus Design Challenge which first appeared in Issue 7 of *Traditional Quiltworks* was born. Since then, my students and I have made hundreds more quilts and you'll see many fresh, new designs on the pages of this book. You'll also get the basics of the easy sewing system, complete with step-by-step photos.

We'll start in Chapter 1 with the simplest of coloring schemes for the pyramid units (I prefer to call them design units rather than blocks because they are triangular rather than square). You'll learn how to sew them quickly. In Chapter 2 you'll see lots of design ideas you can play with and get instructions for assembling the units into a quilt. Once you're familiar with these basics, you'll be ready to move on to the variations in Chapter 3. There you'll find that cutting and sewing the units is the same, but coloring them is different. This means exciting and unique looks for your quilts!

I believe you'll find the array of quilts showcased here inspiring. Playing with pyramid units is fun, challenging and incredibly simple. If you've been avoiding this design because of the 60° angles and bias edges, you're in for a pleasant surprise. I find the pyramid design units to be some of the most "forgiving" I have ever sewn. It's actually the bias edges that make them so. To ensure success, take the time to read the instructions and helpful tips on how to cut and work with the units before you begin. Then relax, start piecing and have fun!

Sharyn

CONTENTS

CHAPTER 1

THE EASY SEWING SYSTEM

The basic pyramid design unit you'll make is a large triangle composed of four smaller triangles. The four small ones are made from four different fabrics that are similar in value. Let's talk about how color and value relate to these pyramid units. When the word color is used, you think of specific hues such as red, blue, green or purple. When the word value is used, think how light or dark that color is. We'll group fabrics in three value categories—light, medium and dark. The fabrics you choose for each category can be one color or many different colors, as long as they are similar in value.

1- Different purple prints in similar values illustrate a good selection of fabrics for pyramid units in one value group.

2-These different purple prints are dissimilar in value. They would *not* work well in the same pyramid units.

3-Different color prints in similar values illustrate a good selection of fabrics for pyramid units.

SUPPLY LIST

- Assorted print fabrics in dark, medium, and light values
- Rotary cutter and mat
- Sewing machine
- A clear plastic triangle with 30°, 60° and 90° angles and the longest side equalling 6" or a 60°-angle quilter's triangle

DIRECTIONS

- Choose 6 dark, 6 medium and 6 light fabrics. For example, you might select 6 dark blue, 6 medium blue and 6 light pink fabrics. You can choose any colors but make sure each group of 6 is similar in value.
- Cut a 3"-wide strip from selvage to selvage from each of the fabrics. Group the strips by like values. These 3" strips will yield 99 units (33 each of dark, medium and light) which finish 4 1/2" tall and 5 1/4" wide.

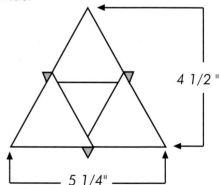

TIP: You can purchase an inexpensive triangle where school or office supplies are sold. They come in a variety of sizes.

TIP: This number of strips will make enough dark, medium and light units for a crib-size, wall or lap quilt. Here's the beauty of "working scrap" for this design. When each strip is cut from a different fabric, you can make a larger quilt simply by cutting more dark, medium, and/or light strips to make more units. You'll never run out of fabric or have to worry about how much fabric to buy!

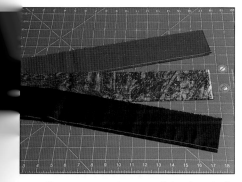

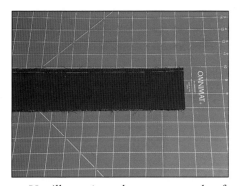

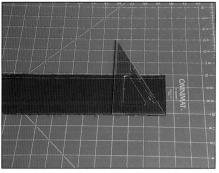

- Set your sewing machine's stitch length at 12 to 14 stitches per inch.
- Beginning with any one of the three value groups (dark, medium or light), select two strips and place them right sides together. Sew them along one long edge, using a 1/4" seam allowance. Sew all of the strips together in pairs in this manner, keeping similar values together. Clip the threads between the pieced strips and group them by value. You will have 3 dark, 3 medium and 3 light pieced strip pairs. The photo shows the dark strips.

- You'll notice that one end of each pieced strip is even, while the other is uneven due to differences in fabric widths. Working with the pieced strips from one value group at a time, place the even end of one pair toward the right edge of the cutting mat if you are right handed and toward the left edge if you are left handed. The seamline should be toward the top of the mat, away from you. Layer the remaining two pieced strip pairs on top of this one, placing the seamlines together and keeping the even ends together.

- Position the triangle on the pieced strips so that the 60° angle is closest to the corner of the even end and points toward the hand you hold the rotary cutter in. The short edge of the triangle should be closest to you.

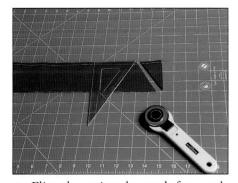

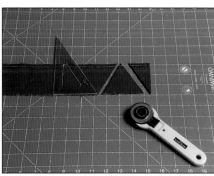

- Cut along the diagonal edge of the triangle, through all six layers of fabric.

- Flip the triangle end for end, aligning the short side with the raw edges of the strips. The 60° angle should be exactly at the top edge of the strip where you stopped cutting.
- Cut along the diagonal edge of the triangle.

- Continue cutting the layered strips into triangles this way, separating the cut pieces into like units. Some will have a seamline at the base (pieced diamonds) while others will have just a few stitches at the tip of the triangle (single triangles).

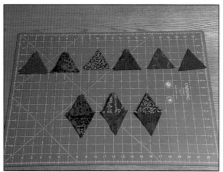

- Pop the stitches at the tips of the triangles and separate them into six piles, each containing single triangles from the same fabric.

TIP: Remember there are lots of bias edges in the units. If you were to iron the units now you would distort them which would make it difficult to assemble them in a flat-lying quilt top. I have found finger pressing prevents distortion and gives more accurate results.

- Carefully finger press the pieced diamonds open, pressing the seam allowances in either direction. Remember the edges are bias, so handle the units carefully. Notice that the seam allowance extends beyond one triangle, forming notches. These notches will be useful when piecing the units and assembling them into a quilt top, so do not trim them off.
- Keeping the seam allowances going in the same direction, separate the pieced diamonds into three piles, each containing units with matching fabrics.

- Select a stack of pieced diamonds and 4 stacks of single triangles cut from different fabrics. Set the remaining 2 stacks aside to be used later.
- Pick up the first pieced diamond and hold it in the palm of your hand so that the seam allowance lies away from your body. Pick up a single triangle from one of the four stacks and place it right sides together with the triangle in the pieced diamond closest to your body. Notice that when you do this, all of the edges and corners are aligned exactly.

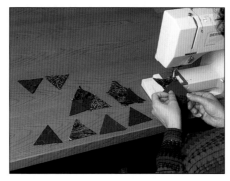

- Sew them from the widest point toward the tip.
- In the same manner, sew triangles to the remaining pieced diamonds in the stack, chain sewing and alternating the stacks from which you select the single triangles.

- Clip these partial units apart and finger press the seam allowances toward the triangle you just sewed. Stack the partial units near your sewing machine, right side up.
- To complete a pyramid unit, you must sew one more single triangle to a partial unit. There is only one place the triangle can go to form the pyramid. Place a single triangle on the partial unit, right sides together, so that the notches match. Sew as before.

- Sew single triangles to the remaining partial units in the stack, alternating the stacks from which you select the single triangles.
- Clip the units apart and finger press the seam allowances toward the single triangle.
- In the same manner, sew pyramid units using the remaining stacks of pieced diamonds and single triangles. For most variety, remember to set aside the two stacks of single triangles that match the pieced diamonds you are working with.
- Complete pyramid units using the remaining two value groups. Now you're ready for some design fun!

A completed pyramid unit.

Six-pointed stars with no set-in piecing—what a deal! I stitched light triangles to dark pieced diamonds in this multi-colored quilt. The "plus" in Pyramids Plus is making quilts with visual surprises like this.

TIP: Your goal is to make many differently colored pyramid units. To make this easier, you'll work with one stack of pieced diamonds and four stacks of single triangles from the fabrics that do *not* match those in the pieced diamond. While you work with one stack of pieced diamonds, simply set aside the two matching stacks of single triangles. That way you'll create lots of different pyramid units without having to do much thinking as you sew. You will have a few single triangles left over for another project.

POINTS TO REMEMBER

• Be sure values within a group of strips are similar.
• When layering pieced strips, place the even ends together toward the side of the mat and seamlines toward the top.
• The 60°-angle of the cutting triangle should always point toward the hand you cut with.
• Use the notches to match pieces for sewing.

CHAPTER 2

DESIGNING AND ASSEMBLING QUILTS WITH BASIC PYRAMID UNITS

Ready for some design excitement? Start playing with the dark, medium and light pyramid units on your design wall. Begin with the simple layout ideas illustrated by the quilts shown here. Remember, because the units have 60° angles, any 60° designs such as Baby Blocks, hexagons or stars are possible. The beauty of working with the triangle shape to create these designs is that you'll use easy, straight-line assembly methods. This means no set-in piecing!

Because the units have equal sides, you can turn them any way you wish to play with the pattern. As you work, you'll discover that most designs will have two straight sides and two zig-zag sides. (This is not true if you arrange the units to create a hexagonal or diamond-shaped quilt.) I recommend filling in the two zig-zag sides with full-size pyramid units or large triangles. Once you sew the units in rows and join the rows into a quilt top, you'll cut away the excess fabric to make these sides straight as well.

It's simple to cut fabric triangles for this use. Just measure one of the pyramid units from the tip to the base (do not include the notch). Then cut a strip of fabric this width. The pyramid units made using the instructions in Chapter 1 should measure 5". Then place the cutting triangle ruler on the strip just as you did when cutting the pieced strips. Be sure the 60° angle is toward the hand you cut with, and the short edge is aligned with raw edge of the strip. Cut along the diagonal edge, flip the triangle end for end and make the second cut. Continue cutting triangles from the entire strip. These triangles will be the exact size and shape of the pieced pyramid units.

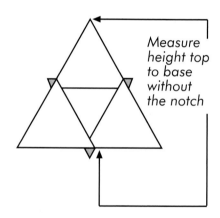

Measure height top to base without the notch

Once you've cut these triangles, try replacing some of the pieced units in your design with them. Using these unpieced triangles provides a resting spot for the eye and larger spaces for quilting designs. They also make it possible to increase the size of your quilt without doing additional piecing.

ASSEMBLING THE QUILT

No matter what design you come up with, each one can be assembled in straight lines. Just follow these steps:
• Start in the upper left hand corner of your quilt. Take the first two pyramids in a row from the design wall to the sewing machine, keeping track of which one was on the left and which was on the right.
• Place them right sides together, matching notches and corners and positioning the triangle that was on the right on top.
• Sew them from edge to edge.
• Open out the top one and finger press the seam allowance toward it.

- Continue adding one triangle at a time this way, always placing the one that was on the right on top and always finger pressing the seam allowance toward it. Pressing this way will result in more notches at each triangle intersection. These notches are going to make sewing of the rows together simple.

- When Row 1 is completed, put it back on the design wall. Sew Row 2 in the same manner.

- Join Row 1 and Row 2, matching the notches. Because of the bias and because you have not ironed the units, you'll find that the units are elastic and resilient. These qualities allow you to slightly ease or stretch the rows as necessary to make them fit together nicely.

- Iron these two rows. I suggest using steam because it will smooth out any small puckers and allow the quilt to lay absolutely flat. Ironing after completing these two rows establishes the finished width of your quilt.

- Sew Row 3 as before. Join it to Rows 1 and 2 and press. Continue sewing rows, joining them to the previous ones and pressing to complete the quilt top.

- To trim the two uneven sides, place your longest rotary cutting ruler on one side. The cutting edge is 1/4" beyond the points of the last triangle you want to remain whole in each row. Carefully cut away the excess and repeat on the other uneven side.

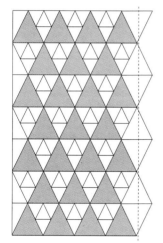

- Add borders as desired, remembering there are lots of bias edges.

Did making one Pyramids Plus quilt whet your appetite? Maybe you feel ready for one of the Pyramids Plus variations. The next chapter will get you going with plenty more design ideas.

▲ *Pyramid units made from light, medium and dark fabric strips form such traditional 60°-angle designs as this Baby Blocks quilt by Sandy Andersen but with no set-in pieces. Sandy sewed units in diagonal rows and used pink setting triangles to make the top and bottom edges even.*

used dark green, medium green and light pink fabrics to make he design units for this Thousand Pyramids quilt. In this traight-row setting, the left and right edges were uneven. I filled hem in with pink and medium green design units and trimmed he quilt to square it up.

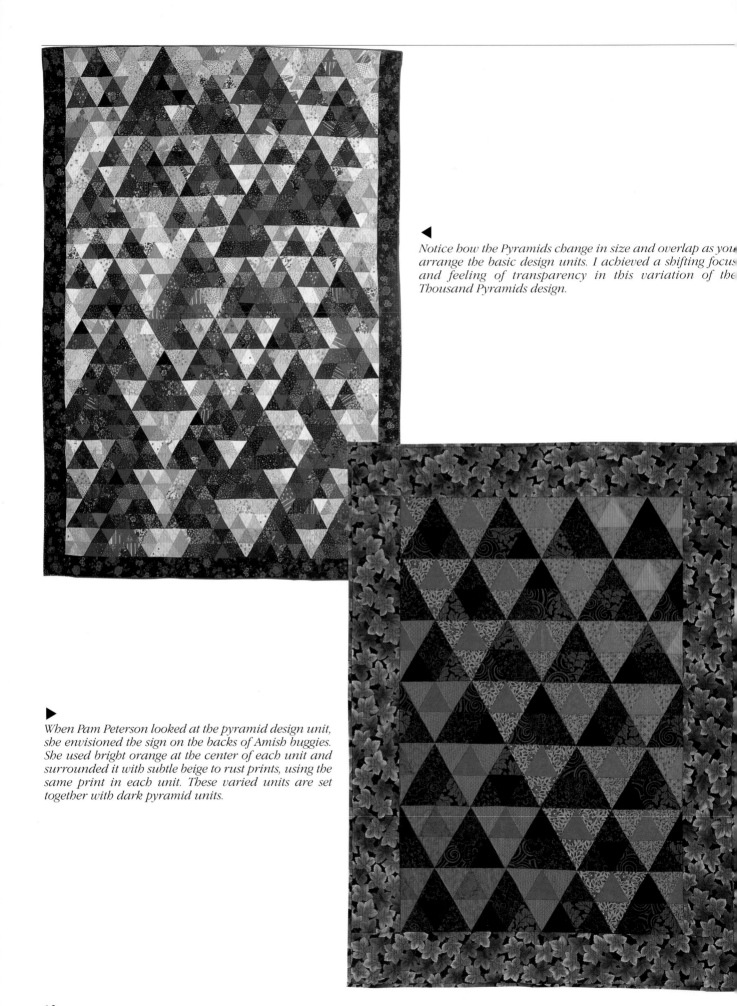

◄ *Notice how the Pyramids change in size and overlap as you arrange the basic design units. I achieved a shifting focus and feeling of transparency in this variation of the Thousand Pyramids design.*

► *When Pam Peterson looked at the pyramid design unit, she envisioned the sign on the backs of Amish buggies. She used bright orange at the center of each unit and surrounded it with subtle beige to rust prints, using the same print in each unit. These varied units are set together with dark pyramid units.*

CHAPTER 3

PYRAMIDS PLUS VARIATIONS

Once you master the construction method for the pyramid units, you can start playing with other coloring options to create brand new designs. Just ask yourself "What If… ." For example, what if you wanted to make a quilt like Laurine Leeke's red, white, and black pyramid star (page 12)? Study the pyramid units to determine how they are different from the basic units you made in Chapter 1.

You probably noticed that Laurine used a white strip in each of the design units. It contrasts sharply with the black and gray tones to create star tips in her design. To achieve this effect, Laurine sewed a white strip to a dark one. Because the white fabric appears only in the pieced diamonds, she didn't need any single white triangles. If you decide to do this, here's a helpful sewing trick. Sew the strips along both long edges. You'll increase the number of pieced diamonds per strip that way. Then cut the necessary single dark triangles from unsewn strips, using the triangle ruler and the same cutting method.

How are other pyramid star quilts like two of mine shown on the front cover and page 7, and page 12 created? The answer is simple. Select the colors or value you want for the star. Use the same sewing method as Laurine did. Sew two strips along both edges and cut them to create the pieced diamonds. Then cut single triangles from the appropriate fabrics to sew to each side of the bottom diamond. Here are some possible arrangements you might use.

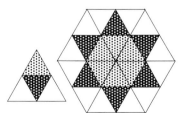

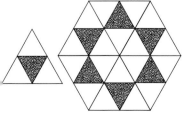

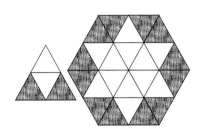

Another of Laurine's quilts (page 13) was inspired by a popular old pyramid design. Now that you know how to create pyramid units, you can make a quilt like hers. Notice that nine small pyramid units are combined with two sizes of unpieced triangles to make the large units. Each small pyramid unit is composed of one dark print and three light print triangles. I suggest starting with 1 1/2"-wide strips to make the small pieced pyramid units and following these steps:

- Stitch a dark and a light strip together along both sides and cut pieced diamonds from this.
- Cut single triangles from other light strips and sew them to the pieced diamonds to complete the pyramid units.
- Measure a unit (without the notch) and cut a strip this width from the dark print.
- Cut triangles from this strip using the triangle ruler.
- Lay out the new unit by placing one unpieced triangle in the center and three pieced pyramid units on the sides. Stitch them together to make a new unit. Make two more units like this.
- Measure the height of this new unit and cut a strip this width from the dark print.
- Cut a triangle from this strip, using a triangle ruler.
- Lay out the final large design unit by placing the unpieced triangle in the center and three of the new units on the sides. Stitch them together.

TIP: For this project, you'll probably need a larger 30°/60°/90° triangle. They are available in many sizes so you can make any size unit.

My "Space Mountain" quilt (shown on the back cover) was also inspired by this old-timey pattern. However, the selection of fabrics resulted in a more abstract design that's a little less predictable. This comparison points out the effect color and fabric choices have on a viewer's perception of a quilt.

I know I'll always be a traditional quilter because I absolutely love the tried-and-true geometric designs. I never tire of seeing the quilts our grandmothers made.

My goal is to be inspired by these old quilts, not to copy them. However, copying is sometimes necessary in order to understand certain technical aspects of construction as in the Pyramid units used in my first Thousand Pyramids quilt. But don't stop there! With the technical support and visual inspiration provided here, you can create your very own originals. I wish you many wonderful quilts... and may some of them be Pyramids Plus!

◄

Can you find the pyramid design unit in Laurine Leeke's exciting star variation? They are composed of one white triangle in the center surrounded by three dark ones. Six units are set together to form the star. A spark of color is added by the red unpieced triangles used to set the hexagonal stars together.

►

I created pastel floating stars by stitching a light and a dark strip from which I cut the pieced diamonds. Then I stitched light triangles to each pieced diamond, placing the dark fabric at the center of the unit. All-light pyramid units lend space to this fun little star design.

◀

An antique quilt inspired this pyramid variation by Laurine Leeke. With today's strip piecing and rotary cutting, it's a sure bet that Laurine made this quilt in less time than our grandmothers could have! What a great showcase for a variety of your favorite prints.

▶

What if you wanted a mixed-scrappy look? Linda Packer used many reproduction prints in the design units of this quilt. Setting them together with unpieced triangles, many in bubblegum pink, gave her quilt a nostalgic feel.

▲
Laurine Leeke made this star-within-a-star design from several combinations of design units. An arrangement such as this makes a lovely wall quilt or medallion for a full-size bed quilt.

▼
Rene Jennings made this holiday table-topper which shows the impact of unit coloration. The entire quilt was pieced from pyramid design units.

▲
Carolyn Smith pieced this dynamic star variation using pyramid units in just two values—light and dark. Notice how many different colors were used in the dark units. The secret to Carolyn's success is that the values are so similar.

Margret Reap chose Baby Blocks for this quilt design because she made it for the birth of her first grandchild. Margret is a master of creative coloring in the pyramid design units.

What if you used dark design units as the background for a spectacular appliqué motif? Rene Jennings made "A Poinsettia for Charlie" as a thank you to her husband for bringing her a poinsettia as an annual holiday gift. The units are so quick to piece that they make a perfect textural background for projects such as this.

Linda Hamby used leftover units from a full-size quilt to piece this little doll-size one.

15

◀ *Linda Hamby used pastel reproduction fabrics to create the design units in her pyramid star variation.*

▶ *Dark stars arranged in a center diamond provide the focus of Joanie Keith's quilt.*

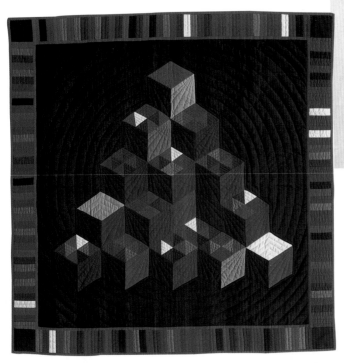

◀ *Patty Barney stitched design units in solid colors and combined them in this Tumbling Blocks arrangement.*